Contents

These Notes are based on the Macmillan Students' edition of *Chosen Poems of Thomas Hardy*, selected and edited by James Gibson.

Foreword

James Gibson's edition of the *Chosen Poems of Thomas Hardy*,
produced for schools, has already become a standard exam-
ination text, and will continue to be one for many years. It
represents Mr Gibson's exhaustive scholarship in the Hardy
field, being in effect a carefully selected contraction of his
The Complete Poems of Thomas Hardy. This latter will remain
the definitive text of Hardy's poetry until Mr Gibson's
massive Variorum Edition appears in the next year or so.

My reason for dwelling on Mr Gibson's texts is to send you,
the readers of these notes, to the *Chosen Poems of Thomas
Hardy* before you read *Brodie's Notes* on that text, for the
Chosen Poems contain a fine introduction to Hardy's poetry,
as well as a chronology of his life and some notes on each
poem: critical, factual, scholarly. You must regard this commentary as a supplement to Mr Gibson's; where he is silent,
the student will perhaps find that I have added to the critical
evaluation of the poem by mentioning its form or structure,
or a particular poetic technique evinced, or that I have
underlined a point made by Mr Gibson, or indicated a
common Hardy theme. Your basic text is the *Chosen Poems*,
your additional source of reference the *Brodie's Notes* on that
text. To Mr Gibson himself I am grateful on many counts;
the first, for the quality of his friendship over a number of
years, and the second for his Hardy scholarship, which has
stimulated me and many like me to a closer reading of the
novels and poems and, indeed, of aspects of the life. Thirdly,
and most important here, I am grateful to him for reading this
book of notes, for correcting it where I am in error, and for
giving it his general blessing as a small extension of his own
work. This is a full acknowledgement of his influence and his
help. *Graham Handley*

For me Hardy is one of our greatest poets. By that I mean that he writes memorably and movingly about many aspects of life, and, in doing so, reveals a richness of observation and a wealth of wisdom which delights and enriches the reader. Whatever kind of man Hardy was in his private life, he shows as a writer qualities of sympathy, kindness, love and awareness which the world now needs more than ever. It is because of this that I rejoice in the success which Hardy's poetry is now enjoying and that I welcome Dr Handley's book. Part of Hardy's appeal is that his poems give the immediate impression of having been written by an ordinary person of great humility and honesty for ordinary people like you and me. They speak directly to us in a language which is often conversational about aspects of life most of us are likely to experience. But this apparent directness and simplicity conceal a mastery of technique which makes Hardy one of our very finest poetic craftsmen. Dr Handley's book will do much to help you appreciate this.

James Gibson, Hawthorn Farm, Dover, 21 August 1977

Introduction

Babette Deutsch, in her *Poetry Handbook*, refers to poetry as 'the art which uses words as both speech and song to reveal the realities that the senses record, the feelings salute, the mind perceives, and the shaping imagination orders'. This is a reasonably definitive statement: to it should be added the qualification that poetry is an individual voice which speaks to individual readers; and that no two readers will respond in exactly the same way to a given set of experiences. The reader of Hardy's verses is set fair, therefore, to taste a variety of moods, descriptions, responses, stories, autobiographical and psychological explorations, love of animals, speculations upon life: make them your own experiences, and not the conveniently adopted views of a critic or teacher. The Notes on each poem are a guide to appreciation. If a poem is read with sensitivity and imagination, with insight and discipline, much more than the Notes tell will be discovered, and the experience will be at first hand, which all experience in literature should be. Perhaps the reader will find himself disagreeing with a particular emphasis or even an interpretation in the Notes. This, unless it results from obstinacy or lack of self-discipline, is a healthy sign, for it marks the beginnings of critical awareness. And once this awareness establishes itself in the mind, confident and balanced judgements will be made; in fact, the art of appreciation will have been learnt.

To the student

Hardy is a poet steeped in local and literary traditions; he is not a modern poet, though the views in his poems, as in his novels, are both modern and timeless. There is a kind of wisdom, of irony, that speaks for all times, and just as Hardy saw divinity in a blinded bird so we see divinity in his poetry, whether it be personal, descriptive, or both. In terms of enlightenment, the man who could subtitle his great novel *Tess of the d'Urbervilles* – in which the tragic heroine is hanged for the murder of her 'lover' – 'A Pure woman faithfully presented', has much to say to our own age. And the man who could conceive *The Dynasts* on the one hand, and write 'In Time of "The Breaking of Nations"' on the other, embraces, like Shakespeare, the permanent truths of life as we know it, and the poems complement the great novels in this signal achievement.

These Notes have not been burdened with too many technical references, since there is a danger that to speak of 'similes and metaphors', for example, will give the reader the impression that he is 'appreciating' the poem concerned. Technical terms are useful only if their *function* is appreciated, if the way they heighten our response to a poem is defined. Consequently, though reference is made to verse forms – for example, ballads and quatrains – to alliteration, onomatopoeia, figurative language, these are *definitions*. They are relevant only in critical commentary when what they achieve is clearly and imaginatively indicated.

Critical commentaries, textual notes and revision questions on the poems

The sequence followed in this commentary is that of the text from pages 27 to 149. The title of the poem is given, followed by some general remarks where appropriate and then a glossary of individual words or phrases, images or techniques. *Note* The student is advised to read James Gibson's notes *fully* before following what is written here.

Poems Mainly Autobiographical

The Field of Waterloo
(from *The Dynasts*)

The Dynasts is written from a range of viewpoints, from the mighty, like Napoleon, to the low, like the Wessex labourer. Here the three-line verses sometimes run into one another, and thus reflect the terrible movement of battle just as the rhythm of the lines reflects the 'thud of hoofs' and the movement of wheels. The poem is imbued with compassion, and the suffering in nature is balanced by the parallel that runs throughout: the senseless suffering of man. The last verse is particularly emphatic here, for the wheat and the flowers that will never reach full growth are a direct comparison with the dead who will not grow on into the fullness of life.

hamlet-roofs i.e. of the villages.
tunnelled chambers ... household ... worm asks i.e. the
  animal world is endowed with human associations, and this gives
  poignancy and a certain pathos to the conception.

guesses him Believes that he is.

foul red rain Blood.

weather-foe As you read on, you will notice that one of Hardy's techniques is the coinage of double-barrelled words which, economically, or poetically or both, extend associations by being joined. His great sympathy for nature, for animals, is very evident here.

greened ... gold ... bud ... bloom Apart from the parallel with man, note the running alliteration which is one of the major facets of Hardy's manner. A close look at the rest of this poem will show how consummately it is used for emphasis – and often how unobtrusively.

One We Knew
(M.H. 1772–1857).

Ballad-form poem of eight four-line verses which initially captures the speed of the dance in the length of its lines, the excitement of her youth, and then varies the line according to the content – reminiscent, nostalgic, evocative of the mood of the past from the point of view of the child on whom his grandmother made such an abiding impression. The poem is a compound of vivid word-pictures and of the *sounds* of the past as well, and the key-line is 'Past things retold were to her as things existent'. Folk-song and ballad, in terms of rhythm and refrain as well as narrative, were of great importance to Hardy.

cots Cottages.

sod Turf.

figures The pattern of the dance.

To choose each other for good There is an inherent simplicity in this, almost a nostalgic wish that youth and the love of youth could be permanent. Note that it was written in 1902, when Hardy's first marriage would be at low ebb.

the King of France Louis XVI, guillotined on 21 January 1793.

the Terror The orgy of bloodshed in the French Revolution which lasted from May 1793 to July 1794.

Bonaparte's unbounded His rise was spectacular, from that of Captain of artillery at Toulon in 1793, first consul by 1799, and consul for life in 1802.

his threats i.e. of invading England.

southern strand South coast.

a small child's shrieking Whether at the lightning, or being beaten, or watching the horse beaten, we are not to know – it is just a vivid evocation of a *felt*, remembered incident.

cap-framed Simple, effective coinage. The headdress would be worn indoors by women at this time.

But rather as one who sees i.e. because they are present to her, as he makes clear in the final verse.

no tongue could hail She is living in her own world of the past, but there is an implication that many she knew are dead, beyond the reach of the 'tongue'.

Past things retold ... Things present ... Note the fine antithetical balance, the consummate economy of expression.

Domicilium

This early exercise already shows Hardy's interest in the past and in nature. A simply expressed poem in blank verse, with a marked influence of Wordsworth in the manner of writing about nature, and a direct echo of some lines in *Tintern Abbey*. Even thus early Hardy had a sense of structure, for the initial descriptions are in short blank-verse paragraphs, which move from the house, the garden, the field and beyond to the 'wilder' scene. The fourth paragraph is longer, since it dwells on the past beyond the past (i.e. his grandmother's as distinct from his own), while the poem closes on the note of the wildness of that distant past. 'A human life', wrote George Eliot, 'should be well rooted in some spot of a native land', and here we have Hardy's roots, simply and lovingly expressed.

sprout a wish Simple personification, but underlining the strong emphatic feeling Hardy has for nature.

box Evergreen shrub.

esculents Something that is eatable; the word is unusual, and here employed with a kind of 'literary' self-consciousness.

Dropped by some bird This sense of time, of continuity, is one of the marks of the 'universality' of Hardy's verse.

A Church Romance
(Mellstock: about 1835)

The sonnet form deftly employed here, with the lightness of touch in the octave balanced by the heavier, longer lines symbolic of age and the changes it has wrought in the sestet. The language is simple, but insistently alliterative, reflecting the music which is so much a part of the romance.

despite Notwithstanding the opposition of (her pride).

hearts' bond ... signed i.e. they were (later) married. But 'bond' carries the half-weight of 'bondage', and is thus ironically used.

Age had scared Romance Heavy personification to underline the burden of the change.

Bowing i.e. playing the viol, but unusually employed as a verbal form here. Note that the sonnet ends with a couplet, an emphatic rounding-off of their lives.

The Roman Road

A short poem of fifteen lines, for the most part in rhyming couplets, but with a refrain line – as in a song, 'The Roman Road' – thus emphasizing the permanence of what is man-made, though the changes which time brings are stressed. The second line echoes another scene description – of man against the background of nature – in Chapter 2 of Hardy's novel *The Return of the Native*, where 'the long, laborious road, dry, empty, and white ... bisected that vast dark surface like the parting-line on a head of black hair'. In Hardy, we always return to the human.

delve Dig.
Visioning i.e. seeing. Another verbal usage.
brass helmed Double-barrelled coinage, with 'helm' being archaic for 'helmet'. Hardy frequently uses archaisms to underline the continuity, the permanence of tradition, which plays so great a part in his philosophy of life.

Childhood among the Ferns

Again the use of the triplets (three-line rhyming verses, though differing from those in 'The Field of Waterloo'), full of descriptive touches which have the immediacy of recall: the scene, the day, the sentiments are recaptured with vividness and yet with an apparently effortless ease of expression and association. It is a moment of childhood with which many of us would feel in sympathy, and because of that its basic appeal lies in the fact that it says for us what we then felt.

sprinkling Notice the effect of the word – immediately arresting in terms of sensation.
tall-stemmed ferns ... tall ferns Hardy is deceptively simple in his use of repetition, here to convey the child's perspective.
lopping Hanging limply.
conned Strictly it means 'studied', and in the sense of storing in the memory, the word fits admirably here.
spray-roofed Fine double-barrelled epithet to convey the effect of the rain.
anon Archaic for 'soon, presently'.
I could live on here thus till death The strongly felt wish to remain within his 'roots' and the experience of nature. Again the influence of Wordsworth is apparent.
queried ... sate Ask myself ... sat. Hardy has used the archaic word here.

And this afar-noised World perambulate Inverted word
order, indicating that he does not wish to grow up. The double-
barrelled coinage contrasts with the peace of the scene, while
'perambulate' shows Hardy's capacity to employ the unusual
word for effect.

The Oxen

Simple ballad-form poem concealing in its deceptive simplicity of language a deep and abiding concern for life and
faith, linking the animal kingdom in its natural humility, with
man in his faith, on the most significant night of the year – and
at the same time expressing the poet's own doubts and yet
his wish to be associated with worship. It is a poignant and
nostalgic poem, deservedly much anthologized. Its universality conveys doubt and hope; a wry appraisal of man's
inherent uncertainty; a moving sense of the loss of the innocent
acceptance that is ours in childhood.

Now they are all on their knees This poem has a fine duality –
the reference is to the oxen, the association with those praying in
church.
elder Note the biblical word, giving a kind of patriarchal touch.
sat in a flock Note the transference of the word from beasts to
people, a further underlining of the duality.
by the embers Favourite Hardy usage, redolent of the warmth
of family life.
hearthside ease Immediate contrast of man with the oxen.
meek mild Note that the words, normally applied to the Virgin
Mary, are deliberately used of the oxen.
there ... then Always the context of time and place stressed.
doubt The word subtly prepares us for the poet's own uncertainty
about his faith.
So fair a fancy i.e. such an imaginative idea.
Hoping The wish expressed is also that of the desire to return to
childhood which nurtured faith in all its simplicity.

The Colour

Note the simplicity of the language, the use of repetition and alliteration, the lilting musical effect in the rhythm and the establishing of a sequence which reflects the changes and movements of life. Verse 1, for example, links white with weddings, verse 2, red with soldiers (i.e. their red coats), verse 3, blue with sailors, verse 4, green with celebrations on May Day, ending with black for death in the last verse. Frequently ballads are in dialogue, and this is a good example of the question-answer balance preserved in so many of them.

Afternoon Service at Mellstock
(About 1850)

Again the four-line verse or quatrain is employed. These are regular, but there is an interesting emphasis in the third line of each verse, where the length of the line matches the singing and the thinking which is a looking away from it. Again, the content is imbued with a wistfulness for the days of childhood, and a pondering on the limitations of the life of thought. It contains some fine things – 'one-voiced' to reflect the unison of the choir, the repetition which echoes the psalm, and some individual coinages characteristic of Hardy's individual manner: 'outpourings', 'psalmings'. Alliteration, a kind of musical accompaniment, runs throughout.

Cambridge New The name of the tune.
whiles Occasions.
swaying like the trees The simile effectively expresses the harmony between man and nature.
mindless Hardy is very fond of 'ess' endings, and coins some of his own, but here what he is conveying is that we do so many things – like singing – without realizing what we are doing or the significance of what is being sung.
psalming Again the use of a noun in verbal form, for emphasis.

A Wet Night

The writer records his experiences of a wet night, feeling his own hardship in the walk through the rain, but pondering on how his forebears took such a thing for granted as part of the routine of their lives. This sonnet, instead of ending with an emphatic closing couplet, has its sestet with alternate rhymes which somehow reflect the ongoing nature of past experience.

rain-shafts riddling Hardy often describes rain, but here the usage implies force – for instance 'arrows' initially – and the alliteration is as continuous as the rain itself. 'Riddling' means 'as through a coarse sieve'.

clams me, mire-bestarred Good combination of the real and the poetic – 'clams' meaning 'clogged with dampness', while the second indicates the mud and the glistening drops of rain on it.

shades Darkness, gloominess.

calendared Again a Hardy coinage, meaning 'to be recorded' and remembered.

sires i.e. forebears.

beset, ere … shapen Note the use of archaisms, words that are appropriate here, since Hardy is dealing with the past; and here meaning 'happened', 'before' and 'made' respectively.

toils as trifles mere i.e. labourings, strivings as everyday occurrences. Note that by inverting the word-order ('trifles mere') Hardy has avoided the cliché.

The Self-Unseeing

Ballad in much shorter lines in which particular moments of the past are recalled. The alliterative effects are finely judged; the soft 'f's of the first verse giving way to the 'd' and 'b' of the last, which fit the joy of the experience and the dance. The language is simple, again until the last verse, where there is a temporarily heightened usage, 'emblazoned' to qualify the then-unrealized ecstasy.

dead feet Hardy has transferred the epithet with economical force
– feet that are *now* dead.

emblazoned This is the heightened word – strictly speaking it
means 'to adorn with heraldic devices', but more commonly to
'celebrate' or 'extol'.

Yet we were looking away! The exclamation shows how
important the phrase is – Hardy is registering the fact that they
did not realize how wonderful the moment was. Perhaps his own
eyes were on the future.

Old Furniture

The play of the imagination, the influences and associations of
memory, ultimately end in a self-denigratory conclusion, but
throughout the poem there is the mastery of an unusual verse
form (five-line), which ends in each case with a short and
emphatic statement. The now familiar nostalgia is apparent,
but the last verse gives the poem a somewhat different slant to
those we have read hitherto.

fashioning Style, make.

As in a mirror a candle-flame This is a fine verse which gives
the perspective of the mind's eye in memory – clear in focus
though the outlines may be progressively dimmer.

A foggy finger This poem is strongly alliterative, but this is one
of the fainter images in the mirror of memory, hence the use of
the adjective 'foggy'.

fingers are dancing Subtle association, for the viol set people
dancing.

My father's Note the implication of the personal and universal
here.

cut ... gut Note the brief hard sounds of the rhymes, which echo
the crispness of the playing.

in fits Abbreviation for 'in fits and starts' i.e. every 'now and
again'.

stark Quite, wholly – very effective, sudden usage here.

Well, well ... But sink away Paraphrased, this means that there is no time in the present to dwell on the past; those who do nothing but reminisce or live in the past should either get on with life or pass quietly away. Hardy's tacit implication is ironical, almost self-pitying, in view of his own chosen association with the past that made him: the places, the people, the things.

To Lizbie Browne

This is an exquisite song, shot through with the suggestion of what might have been that characterizes so much of Hardy's verse. Again the lightness is deceptive, for it covers an experience hitherto unvoiced; and the major part of what was *not* said is recaptured again in the next poem. There is a fine balance here between what is remembered, what is hypothetical, what happened and what might have happened. The result is a lyric of surpassing wistfulness, a melodic memory given permanence by being cast in words. The lines are short, for the time of youth and opportunity is short; the repetition and the refrain show how often the image of the subject has been repeated in the poet's mind. The subtle variations within the constriction of the verse form show Hardy's ingenuity, his feeling for the play of words and the associations set up by them. Strangely, with all the nostalgia, it is a poem of youth: the subject a child of nature; the song sprinkled with an alliterative flair that makes it easy on the tongue and the ear.

archly wile i.e. coyly cunning.

glance-giving Once more the economic coinage which says so much so directly.

Bred out of doors The simple recall is to the enhancing simplicity of nature.

By stealth to one i.e. secretly (to him).

swift ... slow A play on 'The race is to the swift', here with ironic self-regret.

Girls ripen fast True, and the image again links her with the natural background of her 'ripening'.

Faintheart in a Railway Train

Very similar to the previous poem in theme – ironic appraisal of what might have been – but here based on an even more precarious incident. Two five-line verses, with a repetitive opening to each line of the first verse; and a stressed sequence which goes from town, to nature, to the girl seen. This leads naturally to the second verse, where he lacks the courage and enterprise to get out of the train and approach the 'radiant stranger'; and the final exclamation is one of regret.

smirch Stain.
in my search for a plea i.e. trying to find an excuse (for speaking to her).

At a Lunar Eclipse

This poem is a sonnet, the first part of the octave (lines 1–4) being descriptive of the eclipse itself; the second (lines 5–8) questioning the relationship between this manifestation and the earth as he, the poet, knows it. In the sestet, – which is divided into two three-line questions – and throughout the final part, the contrast between the shape of the earth and its inward turmoil is stressed. The poem is thus tightly-structured, following a logical, if distressing, sequence.

monochrome i.e. in one colour.
sun-cast symmetry i.e. as round and as smooth as the sun, which is responsible for casting the earth's shadow on the moon.
form ... profile ... brow Notice that the earth is personified, its reality being given human shape by association. The movement from the personal to the all-embracing (see 'continents' in the next line) is one of the features of the poem.
yon arc i.e. the eclipse.
Nation at war with nation i.e. the affairs of mankind, warfare, thinking, being brave or beautiful, are of small moment when seen against the vastness of space.

Neutral Tones

Perhaps the finest evocation of a mood in Hardy's verse, achieved by a consummate re-creation of a scene and an atmosphere consonant with the mood of the lovers. The first verse sets the scene, which is unusual in that the colours are 'neutral' rather than positive; it prepares us for the exchanges, largely unverbalized, between the lovers. The second verse is characterized firstly by the silence of the looks between them, and then – a superb technical achievement – the strained nature of the words when they do speak. Here the word-order underlines the nature of the experience they are suffering. The third verse describes the dead smile and the 'grin of bitterness', while the final verse shows the poet, in the light of experience, looking back on the sharp outlines of a scene which will recur, with all that it symbolizes, in his memory.

chidden Scolded or rebuked, archaic here. Notice that the term is strengthened in line 15 to 'God-curst'.

tedious riddles The implication is of unanswered questions, the tiresome exploration of their situation.

On which lost the more by our love The exact meaning is not clear, but the strain and tedium of the exchanges is reflected in the uncertain word-order.

Like an ominous bird a-wing A simile which indicates the death of love, the bird being a bird of prey. The scene is thus symbolic of a tortured good-bye.

wrings with wrong Note the fine alliteration to stress the squeezing out, torturing nature of the experience.

In a Eweleaze near Weatherbury

Fine lyrical touch from Hardy as, at the age of fifty, he recaptures once more the essential nature of an early love-experience. The form is simple, with three eight-line verses, each having alternate lines rhyming. He dwells on the fact that, though he has changed in terms of age, in basic response to life he is unchanged. He would still worship Beauty, though he records wryly that it would not reply to him in the language of past love.

Eweleaze A grass field or down stocked with sheep.
kindled gaily Love's fitful ecstasies i.e. happily moved me to love her.
feature ... fantasies i.e. the aspect in my dreams.
never-napping A quietly effective coinage – Time never rests or 'naps'.
I'd go ... Beauty I'd do anything. The personification of Beauty appears to refer to youthful love and everything associated with it, i.e. it is both particular and general.
balm the breeze i.e. sweeten it.
Thine for ever i.e. I will be yours (true to you) for ever. And when he dies he will be able to look back with enjoyment.

Great Things

A light-hearted romp expressing great joy in life, in drink, cycling, dancing and love; the final verse summarizing these 'great' things to be had before death. It is a song dependent on repetition and the refrain, its zest being its main quality.

hostelry i.e. public house.
flits like one a-wing i.e. comes towards me lightly like a bird. Compare the image with the one used in the previous poem.
One will call, 'Soul, I have need of thee' i.e. the onset of death.
Joy-jaunts i.e. drinking and cycling.

'When I set out for Lyonnesse'

The very name of Lyonnesse has legendary associations, for it was supposedly the scene of many incidents in the Arthurian story and in the romances of Tristan and Iseult. It is very important in Cornish tradition and folklore, and all this is present in the *language* of Hardy's fine lyric. Although it is about a personal journey, the use of archaisms and the choice of words like 'lonesomeness' and 'fathomless' remind one of the timeless quality of the scene. In fact, the past informs the present, almost as if a knight has gone in quest of his lady and won her love. The verses are of six lines each, repetition and alliteration run throughout; the first verse deals with the journey; the second with the guesses at what happened while he was there; and the third registers his return 'With magic in my eyes!'.

bechance Archaic – it really means 'happen' here.
wisest wizard A deliberate invocation of the past and of folklore (perhaps a glance at the legendary Merlin of Arthurian romance).
All marked Everyone noticed.
fathomless i.e. which could not be guessed at.

The Sun on the Bookcase
(Student's Love-song: 1870)

Two seven-line verses, the first purely descriptive of the room and of nature outside. The second is rather different in tone, arguing finally that time has not been wasted; for when the poet has achieved what he has to he will be able to claim his loved one. It has none of the elevation of the previous poem – the journey is of the imagination – but it does record an experience common to many who are separated.

the boiling ball i.e. the sun.
imaged i.e. formed the image of, pictured in one's mind's eye.
anon Presently (archaic).
alway Always (archaic).

'We Sat at the Window'
(Bournemouth, 1875)

Two eight-line verses, with varying length of line and an elaborate rhyme scheme: the first descriptive of the day, which sets the mood; the second descriptive of the couple as they reflect the mood. It is a kind of domesticated 'Neutral Tones', but completely lacking the intensity and the emotional tautness of that poem. Nevertheless it conveys well the emotional, sympathetic dissonance between the couple very well, and might be contrasted with the earlier poem; it is almost as if the habit of life together has muted any natural outgoing.

like silken strings Note the various descriptions Hardy gives of rain – 'silken' perhaps conveys domestic bondage or intensity.

witless things But the image is ironic – the couple themselves have 'wits' but don't use them to each other, and the couple are unhappy in their silence and passivity.

We were irked by the scene Note the longer line as the poem becomes reflective.

waste One of Hardy's favourite words to describe the inability to realize fully a moment in time and to enjoy it.

A January Night
(1879)

A short poem with two themes: first, the description of the night outside; then the supernatural association of the night with the man recently dead. Three verses, alternate lines rhyming, with a vivid personification of nature at the beginning (not unlike a sick person in its outburst); and the implication that perhaps nature reflects in its agony the agony of the dead man's spirit. Very simple language, ending with the enigma of ignorance.

smites Note the heavy alliterative effects and also those of personification, so that the wind and the rain become a creature.

Writhes This word sets in train the 'dread' associations which the
poet cannot account for.

The Last Signal
(11 October 1886) A Memory of William Barnes

The technical qualities are fully indicated in this note
by *JG*. William Barnes (1800–86) wrote many poems whose
subject matter overlap Hardy's own, and throughout his
verse runs a rich love of nature and a strongly compas-
sionate tone. Hardy edited the Select *Poems of William Barnes*,
choosing what to include in the edition himself. The lyrical
tone, but with considerable technical virtuosity, predomi-
nates; *The Milkmaid O' The Farm* is a good example, a simple
Tess situation without the tragedy.

And dark was the east The inverted word order perhaps
symbolizes the end of a life.
athwart Across.
grave-way A fine brief coinage to indicate 'on his way to be
buried'.

Shelley's Skylark
(The Neighbourhood of Leghorn: March 1887)

Shelley's 'Ode to a Skylark' ('Hail to Thee, blithe spirit!')
is imbued with the poet's individual lyrical meditations.
Hardy, by way of contrast, speculates on the bird that in-
spired them: the one bird, of course, symbolizing the many.
The poem is in quatrains, has some superb turns of phrase but,
it must be confessed, some rather obvious literary 'conceits', or
far-fetched references.

oblivious eyeless i.e. unseen and unknown, the term almost
echoed at the end of the first verse.
through times to be i.e. all time.

when piped farewell i.e. sang its last notes.

throbs in a myrtle's green Imaginative phrase, the skylark 'feeding' the evergreen shrub, with white-scented flowers, sacred to Venus.

the coming hue/Of a grape Again the imaginative association, 'coming' finely conveying the development of ripeness.

Ecstatic heights We might note that the heights are the skylark's too, or, in the words of Shelley, 'That from Heaven or near it ...'

At the Pyramid of Cestius near the Graves of Shelley and Keats
(1887)

Although this poem is in four-line verses, it is technically striking because of the very long third line in each verse which contains the substance of the poet's thought. The opening has an echo ('Who is Sylvia, what is she?' from Shakespeare's early comedy *The Two Gentlemen of Verona*), and the poet seems to be trying to achieve a balance between the conversational tone and a certain elevation required by the subject.

One thought alone brings he Inverted word order, perhaps reflecting history's inverted decision on Cestius.

Whose purpose was expressed The pyramid was designed to glorify the memory of Cestius, but instead it glorifies the memory of two poets unknown to him.

history-haunted Keats, too, employed the double-barrelled epithet, so Hardy has chosen appropriately here the coinage conveying the mixed history of Rome from pre-Christian times.

matchless singers i.e. Keats and Shelley.

– Say, then Note the admirable, clear-cut language of this verse, as compact as the pyramid, as clear as the fame of the two poets.

The Division

Moving love poem and, though the physical distance between the lovers is not as important as 'that thwart thing', it is ironic that it was also the distance to Lyonnesse. Each of the verses is an exclamation of anguish, the weather being almost incidental to the inward tumult. The poem is characterized by unusual words: 'severance', 'thwart' and the archaic 'betwixt'; but in terms of balance and passion it is a poignant lyric. There is, too, a terrible finality about it.

A Broken Appointment

Again the poignant note is sounded, but here the emphasis on form tends to detract from the sincerity of utterance. The first and final lines of each of the two verses are the same, giving the effect, almost, of a foreshortened *rondeau* (see for example Leigh Hunt's 'Jenny Kissed Me'). Having said that, let us add that the theme is vital to any understanding of Hardy the man, the 'lovingkindness' so rightly stressed in James Gibson's note. There is therefore a high sense of loss, not in the conventional sense, but of loss to the human spirit which does not live in 'lovingkindness'.

hope-hour Another fine economical coinage to underline anxiety.

love alone can lend you loyalty The core of Hardy's belief – and note the exquisitely soft alliteration in which it is expressed.

time-torn See 'hope-hour' (line 7) for the same effect of racked with anxiety.

The Impercipient
(At a Cathedral Service)

In effect, this is a hymn in defence of doubt, sensitively using some of the associations of faith to mark the writer's own consciousness, regret and natural humility. It is a beautifully balanced poem, but there is a moving sense of isolation about it too – as if the man who stands in a congregation is even more conscious of his difference as a non-believer than if he had never gone to church! Here, Hardy's known affiliation with what is traditional should also be taken into account. The structure – effectively alternate lines rhyming, short and long – is brought to an abrupt end in the final two lines; as abrupt, one might say, as death.

mirage-mists i.e. delusions.

consigned i.e. delivered.

Abides i.e. remains.

I am like a gazer There is some difficulty here. The verse seems to mean that, to some, the wind in the trees will symbolize the sea – because of its noise, associations. There is perhaps even the idea of a mast at sea, made from a like tree. Others, like Hardy, will merely see a tree and nothing beyond. Some see evidence of their faith everywhere; others, like the poet, merely see things for what they are.

upfingered Again the economical expressive coinage.

But for the charge i.e. the poet resents being taxed with the accusation that he would rather not believe in divine goodness, for it is not true – it would be tantamount to saying that a bird that has no wings deliberately seeks out the earth, whereas in fact it cannot fly above it anyway.

disquiet Doubt, uncertainty. Note the superb economy of the ending, the 'Rest shall we' which is synonymous with the eternal rest – death.

The Going of the Battery
Wives' Lament (2 November 1899)

Ballad with internal rhyme and the regular rhythm mentioned in the previous sentence, the style somewhat reminiscent of the Victorian minor poet Thomas Hood. The final effect is that of stoicism in the face of adversity: moved though Hardy was, the sentiments are idealized rather than realistic.

Light in their loving i.e. flitting, not stable or true.

the South Sea Presumably the Mediterranean, or any sea that has to be crossed.

living things seeming there The idea is extended in the next line, but the terrible irony is that they are takers of life.

tar-cloths ... upmouthed Note again the effect of the 'humanizing' of what is made to destroy, part of an ironic overtone.

blank ... prophetic An extension of the idea above. They are 'blank' at the moment.

Hand i.e. God.

Other and graver things i.e. the fear (in the small hours of the morning) that their men will not return.

Drummer Hodge

The contemplation of death in war, the fate of the ordinary man, is the theme here. There is a strikingly individual vocabulary and touch employed in this poem, though the structure – three six-line verses with alternate lines rhyming – has been used in previous poems. The simplicity emphasizes the sudden simplicity of death. Nature and the heavens provide the background and foreground to the poem; for they are permanent, whereas man's life is transitory.

They throw in Notice the lack of dignity, undoubtedly used as a contrast with the formal pomp common at funerals of those who die at home in peacetime.

kopje ... veldt ... Karoo All emphasize the foreignness to Hodge.

Hodge The name is traditionally typical of the English country labourer. Implicitly Hardy is comparing his natural occupation with where he ends; unnaturally, for this earth is foreign to him. And, as we see from the previous verse, 'foreign' constellations are above him.

unknown Hardy is fond of using the negative, this time with sardonic irony: Hodge, being dead, cannot 'know' where he is buried.

strange-eyed constellations There is a clever transference of the double-barrelled 'strange-eyed' here, since they would only be strange to the dead soldier if he could see them. A further underlining of the pathos of the simple man dying far from all he knows.

The Man He Killed

Another aspect of the theme of war: the short four-line verses virtually in the shape of a monologue; the whole presenting the ironic but essentially true idea that a man does not hate his foe, he merely kills him. Behind this there is the additional social comment – the casual way that men enlist, or the poverty that forces them to do so.

to wet i.e. drink.
Just so There are three breaks in two lines here – a subtle indication that the soldier has difficulty in reasoning out the rights of the matter of war.
'list i.e. enlist, join up.
Off-hand like i.e. casually, without thinking.
traps trappings, bits and pieces.
quaint ... curious Both words are inadequate to describe the horror of war, and therefore carry their own irony.
where any bar is Once more the reversed word order is effective, for war itself reverses standards.

The Darkling Thrush

Four eight-line verses, though effectively each verse consists of two quatrains with alternate lines rhyming. The poem is rich in imagery, personification and contrasts. Its focus is on the landscape as compared with the one thing that is not consonant in mood with it – the song of the thrush. The latter is redolent of hope, while the landscape, frost-bound, is desolate. In the first verse the poet, alone, contemplates the scene; while in the second the compelling atmosphere overcomes him so he is 'fervourless', deprived of animation. Verse three marks the sudden transition, the joyful song of the bird belying its appearance. In verse four the poet ponders on the contrast between song and scene and the unknown and animating spirit of the thrush.

Frost was spectre-grey Notice the personification and the fact that it is nearly night, when spectres might appear – an imaginative connection in the poet's mind, since it anticipates the 'spectre' of the thrush.

dregs i.e. sediment, what is left; sap fallen to its lowest level.

scored Cut or scratched.

Like strings of broken lyres The simile is particularly apt, since there is no music in the scene until the thrush begins to sing.

haunted Reiteration of ghostliness and death.

The land's sharp features ... his death-lament These four lines, a sequence of personification, make the landscape 'dead' by using traditional associations of burial – the crypt and the lament, for example – and there is a fine running alliteration of hard 'c's which are as crisp and stiff in sound as is the frost in reality.

The ancient pulse Notice that the personification is continued, to stress the absence of any life-force in the scene.

fervourless The effectiveness here is by contrast with the landscape, since fervour means 'heat' or 'passion'.

At once Note the clever use of rising rhythm to convey exultation.

evensong This simple word, evocative of Christian worship, invests the thrush with a spiritual quality.

blast-beruffled Splendid coinage to indicate the survival powers of the thrush against the winter storms.

fling his soul This means simply to 'sing with all his heart', but 'fling' is a splendid choice of word since the thrush himself has been 'flung' by the 'blast'.

carolings Carols are sung in praise of the birth of Christ; there is a touch of irony in its usage here, for there appears to be nothing to praise in the landscape, though again the spiritual quality of the bird's song is evident.

terrestrial Earthly, contrasting with the spiritual.

blessed Hope 'Hope springs eternal in the human breast', wrote
  Pope, but Hardy chooses to stress the bird's intuitive sense of the
  coming of spring. The mood of the poet is sombre, as unhopeful
  as that of the landscape, whereas the bird's song is redolent of joy.

To an Unborn Pauper Child

Birth is a favourite subject for poets, and the interested
student might like to compare Hardy's fine poem here with
Louis MacNeice's ominous 'Prayer Before Birth' or Philip
Larkin's 'Born Yesterday'. The verse form – six-line stanzas
with two short lines in the middle – is finely controlled. The
first verse is an invocation to the unborn child, urging it not
to come into a world of suffering and apprehension. Verse
two extends this idea by asserting that nothing can be changed
by the coming child. Subtly we are reminded of the child who
did come and who wrought change: Christ. The third verse
tacitly asks the question of the child: if it knew all there was
to know about life, would it accept it for what it (life) is?
Verse four deals with the inevitability of the birth anyway;
and verse five underlines the poet's compassion and at the same
time registers his acknowledgement that man cannot change
anything. Yet the final verse is optimistic in tone: the child
may find 'Health, love, friends, scope' despite its start in life.
In many ways this is similar to the previous poem: there the
landscape contrasted with the bird's song; here the fears and
sufferings of life are finally diminished in an upsurge of faith
in humanity.

wombed souls i.e. those conceived but not yet born.
terrestrial chart i.e. earthly pattern of life.
locked sense i.e. because shut in the womb, unable to feel, hear,
  see what is outside.
pending plan i.e. what will happen.
the common lot to rare i.e. to change the common lot of

mankind (suffering and unhappiness) to the rare (happiness and fulfilment).

unreasoning Relying on our belief that life will be happy rather than our reason which tells us it will not.

sanguine Hopeful, confident.

Shut out that Moon

A finely sustained cynical assertion of the changes wrought by time. The moon is traditionally associated with romance and love, but the poet chooses to reject its past associations – the outside, freedom of love and life – and to accept, or apparently accept, imprisonment in the room, which is perhaps synonymous with domesticity. It is, too, a sad lament for joys now gone.

Before our lutes were strewn i.e. before the joys of life – the songs and dances of youth – (became dusty).

dew-dashed Fine coinage, indicating Hardy's almost casually-poetic observation.

Brush not the bough Note the fine contrast employed in this stanza with the previous one – there the contemplation of the heavens, here that of nature and the past associations of love. Unobtrusive indication that the room is 'shared' – but only in person, not in spirit. Note the change in this verse from the imperative which has opened the first three.

Too tart the fruit i.e. sour.

After the Last Breath

Not the conventional death-bed scene, but a moving and constrained reaction to the aftermath of death. It is a typically individualistic treatment, and the verse form (yet another variant of the four-line stanza with a short end-stopped line at the conclusion), is handled with deft assurance. It is noteworthy that the first two verses are simply, directly expressed, while the third lists the medical trappings which were ineffectual and now have no use. The last two verses express death as a kind of freedom, as compared with life for those who live on.

Our morrow's anxious plans Note the ironic concept of death the great leveller as compared with the petty affairs of men, for so often we plan in vain.

its silly face Note how effective the personification is, ironically, *after* the death.

savours i.e. tastes, strictly speaking. But here 'appears' or 'seems' would perhaps be better.

by littles Unusual term meaning 'by degrees'.

Outshapes i.e. appears.

The Convergence of the Twain
(Lines on the loss of the *Titanic*)

James Gibson's commentary precludes the necessity of any introduction here, except perhaps the added note that the poem has a resonance and elevation more commonly associated with an ode.

tidal lyres i.e. the tides in their regularity of movement are compared to the strings, the rhythmic plucking of which produce melody.

grotesque, slimed Note the effect achieved by the single words, each obliquely conveying the tragedy.

What does this vaingloriousness down here? The speaking fish are a moment of bathos, rare in Hardy, who usually manages to sustain his tone.

In shadowy silent distance Note how the longer line 'grows' like the iceberg which is being described.

august Ironically used word in the light of the disaster.

At Tea

Shorter than a sonnet; yet in two halves that are rather like that form. A moment in time recaptured, with the strongly suggestive 'might have been', which, as we have seen earlier, forms an important part of Hardy's appraisal of passing situations. The verse is limpid and simple, reflecting the smooth gloss that covers the reality, the last line providing an unvoiced indication of inner feelings.

that she fills an envied place i.e. she is being complacent, secure.

abloom i.e. with excitement, perhaps in the knowledge that she is still loved; or in the knowledge of the shared secret of the past with the husband. Or perhaps she has taken particular trouble with her appearance, to outshine her married rival.

And he throws her a stray glance The unexpectedness is half the effect, the other half lying in the deception and its corollary – the future of the marriage.

By Her Aunt's Grave

Superb short poem, finely ironic, cynical (but true) in its appraisal of a kind of human nature; the irony lies in the pathetic 'respectability' of old age (which saves for a headstone and thus achieves respectability in death); as distinct from the heartlessness of youth, which spends in one evening the money saved over eighty weeks. The breaking of trust is thus thematic here, and there is the additional implication of the man influencing the girl, perhaps not merely to an abuse of trust, but towards seduction and the abuse of her too. The dialogue gives the poem a certain dramatic force and immediacy; but note the brilliantly conveyed effect in the last line, which is not in speech but in commentary.

In the Cemetery

A sonnet that is an ironic comment on human nature and the reality of death, but with a finely sympathetic penetration into the individual need to let go, to release emotion which has a focus in the loved ones who are dead. Again the use of speech provides a certain poignant force. The comment also embraces the natural tendency towards argument and under-pins the possessiveness inherent in most of us.

like sprats in a tin A superb simile to define the anonymity of death, its essential sameness which, ironically, cannot be grasped by the individual mourner.

And as well cry over a new-laid drain The psychology of this is unerring – and in addition there is the comment that we weep over what appears, for example the grave and the flowers which symbolize the beloved, rather than the reality which we cannot see.

The Going

This opens the sequence of poems which have reference to the death of Emma Hardy. The technical mastery, with its poignant variation of tone and the blending of a distant past with the stultifying recent one is the hallmark of mature poetic expression.

close your term here A euphemistic way of describing what the poet finds so unacceptable – death.

ever anon i.e. presently. But note the force of 'ever'.

lip me Note the softness, almost tenderness that the word implies.

morning harden ... Unmoved, unknowing The suggestion is that all personal qualities possessed by the day are dead – as she is; and it is finely descriptive as well.

Had place i.e. had taken place.

for a breath i.e. for a moment (as fleeting as a breath).

Life unrolled i.e. this was the best time of our lives.

vanishing Another euphemism for death, but emphatic of the suddenness and completeness of the 'going'.

I seem but a dead man held on end ... would undo me so The moving quality of these lines is apparent – the broken phrases are as sighs or tears; the breaking down after the sustained expression, quite dignified; the grief; the regret for the wasted years. And perhaps the most poignant part of this is the self-knowledge that has come with death: the moving evidence that we do not know our innermost thoughts or feelings until personal tragedy reveals them to us.

The Haunter

This is almost a reply to the previous poem, for in one leap of the spectral imagination, so to speak, Hardy has written the poem in the wished-for words of his dead wife. The eight-line verses are a recurring pattern of rhyme, and there is a fine fluidity about the whole poem, almost as if the essence of the spirit has been captured and distilled in a light flow of expression. The poignancy lies in the inability to communicate between the two worlds – that of the supposed spirit of the dead with that of the continuing cycle of the living. The same note of regret, of time wasted in the past, is apparent throughout this poem as in the previous one.

where the past is all to him The phrase 'haunted' Hardy, and recurs with a slight variation in 'The Voice'.

O tell him The whole of this verse is really a poignant cry not only from the 'haunter', but from the poet, for reassurance of continuing love, a love not fully appreciated in life.

The Walk

Two eight-line verses, almost lyrical in tone, but imbued with that quality of wistfulness found in the last two poems. The sense of loneliness and isolation is most marked. The end of the first verse epitomizes what is taken for granted in life; while the end of the second underlines this by the expression of loss. This last line does not rise to a climax of discovery, but rather falls away in a finely expressed understatement; almost as if the poet, by speaking of the 'look of the room', is obliquely uttering what Wordsworth called 'thoughts that do often lie too deep for tears' – thus underlining the fact that Emma is *not* there, but elsewhere.

The Voice

This evocation of 'utter loss' is a vivid recollection, which equates with the wind the voice the poet *wants* to hear, as he stands in a desolate lonely place. The poem is written in quatrains, with a dexterous use of repetition and triple rhymes at the ends of lines, almost as if the echo of the longed-for voice has been captured. Alternate lines rhyme, but the mood is sustained by varying the flow of the verse with lines that stop abruptly in the middle, as the poet's consciousness adjusts itself to the encroachments of the past. It is superbly structured, a piece of technical virtuosity; the long-line first two verses sound the deeps of memory, while the last two short-line verses contract into the present – from the questioning third verse down to the final desolation of the poet as he stands alone in an isolated place, emotionally and mentally stripped by memory.

when our day was fair i.e. when we were happy, when fate smiled on us.
Wind oozing thin Unusual association, for 'oozing' is usually of liquid.

At Castle Boterel

Another thematic exploration of the past and its searing effect upon the present: in seven verses of five lines each, the much shorter line at the close of each verse sometimes running naturally into the next one. Again the poet looks back in time to an excursion taken with his loved one, so that the poem is a mixture of poignant nostalgia on the one hand and the deep pathos of age and acceptance on the other. The mastery of the form is shown by the confident stopping in the middle of the line where appropriate, and the sustaining of a confiding tone of conversational ease.

Something that life will not be baulked of i.e. love.
In that hill's story? A subtly transferred emphasis – the story is
  of the lovers' exchanges – and of many other lovers too.
the transitory in Earth's long order i.e. what passes in life,
  involving change.
for my sand is sinking A poignant recognition of age, that he
  has not long to live, the metaphor being that of the sand in the
  hour-glass.

After a Journey

This is written in four eight-line verses; the theme of a return to the past being given a like actuality to that of the previous poem. The revisit to a place where love and happiness were enjoyed is another expression of constancy, since the final lines assert that

> I am just the same as when
> Our days were a joy, and our paths through flowers.

There is the customary running alliteration and repetition; fine natural observation; the use of archaic and dialect words to stress the past and concrete reality: the recognizable hall-marks of Hardy's manner at the time. Once again we are aware of that unique sense of recall across the years, resulting in the evocation at will of physical description, scene and atmosphere.

twain Two of us.
Time's derision i.e. the mocking laughter because of what they 'wasted'.
mist-bow The spectrum that forms above the spray. Note how cleverly Hardy uses repetition here, the poignant emphasis of 'then'.
flitting Passing lightly, i.e. like a ghost!
the stars close their shutters Effective domestic metaphor applied contrastingly, as it were, to the house of the heavens.
lours Is dark and threatening.

Beeny Cliff
(March 1870–March 1913)

Written in triplets with an insistent rhythm, initially capturing the joyfulness of youth and finally the grandeur of the scene despite the death of the loved one. In terms of sheer richness of colour, depth of association and verbal virtuosity, this poem bears comparison with anything that Hardy ever wrote.

loyally loved me This seems to imply an inequality between them which Hardy remembers, that she loved him *despite* ... It reflects how carefully the words are weighed here.
ceaseless babbling Note how the last word conveys the sounds of the mews.
A little cloud ... And the Atlantic dyed its levels ...
misfeatured Almost a prophetic symbol, the 'clear-sunned' reflecting their love, the above references the obscuring of it in their life, and the next line – 'And then the sun burst out ...' the re-kindling of that love for him later.
balks Note the fine onomatopoeic effect.
And nor knows nor cares for Beeny Certainly nature is permanent and the life of man ephemeral, but here what is

unsaid is as important as what is said – she cannot know or care for the writer either. Note how 'laughs' brilliantly picks up the 'laughed' of line 6.

The Frozen Greenhouse
(St Juliot)

Finely economical poem in short-line verses, again recalling an incident and linking it unequivocally with the present; the changed circumstances; the ironic survival of a thing (the greenhouse) as against the death of the loved one. It is a small sad song, none the less effective because the lilting regret is conveyed with exactitude, and balanced in past and present with an exquisite attention to contrasting details – note that the greenhouse is 'Warm, tight, and gay' while the plants were 'Cold, iced, forgot' – and that both phrases apply equally to the dead woman, in her life and in her death.

On a Discovered Curl of Hair

Another effective simple poem, again evocative of the past and its relation to the present. This time it is written in couplets, with some unusual choices of words and the now familiar balance between the past and the present struck in the two halves of the poem.

dinned Were noisy, but note the onomatopoeic quality of the word.
absentness Fine choice, conveying much more than 'absence', for the length of the word itself looks forward to the 'absentness' that is now permanent for the poet.
For brightest brown have donned a grey i.e. she was grey-haired before she died.
Beams with live brown The word 'live' is the important one, contrasting immediately with the fact of death.

A Night in November

There is a fine imaginative connection between the suffering of man and the suffering of nature in this poem of three quatrains with alternate lines rhyming. The first verse describes the outside tumult of the storm; in the second the tree symbolizes the loss of man; while the third (in which the man touches what the tree has lost – the leaf – and imagines that it is his loved one), brings man into empathy with nature. The result is a poem of succinct identification of mood and atmosphere.

a tree declared to the gloom Personification, but the outside wailing and shaking of the tree – its language if you like – can be imagined.

And saying at last you knew i.e. that he still loved her.

During Wind and Rain

The poem exerts a powerful effect through the associations of memory: each of the four verses having a refrain which takes the form of a lament for the passage of time, the passing of youth and life and the inevitable onset of death. At the end of the poem we realize that the names on the gravestones have moved the poet to journey into the past, for the poem, while focusing on more than one, always has the one – the dead beloved – in mind.

the white storm-birds wing across Just as birds presage a storm, so Hardy uses the image to suggest change and, ultimately, death.

And the rotten rose is ript from the wall Death comes to all things, and the description anticipates the removal of the furniture and fittings when the owners are dead. The power is in the word 'ript'.

Down their carved names This is a reference to the gravestones which mark the final resting place of those described in the poem.

Channel Firing

The student should familiarize himself with the fact that the supposed narrator is a dead man.

altar-crumb i.e. the mouse stealing the consecrated bread.
Blow the trumpet i.e. to summon the dead to judgement.

In Time of 'The Breaking of Nations'

This much-anthologized piece, written in quatrains with alternate lines rhyming, has a timeless universality. It contemplates the tragedy of the First World War, and its theme is quite simply the unchanging nature of the simple things of life – reflected in an agricultural landscape – as distinct from the rise and fall of kingdoms and empires. The tone is wry, ironic, yet imbued with compassion; it throws into sardonic and uncompromising relief the passing glory and pointlessness of war.

annals Historical records, narrative of events year by year.

Ten Years Since

A very simple poetic exercise, but showing amazing facility in rhyming and rhythmic ability for a man of eighty-two. Despite the lightness of touch the regret comes through as the positive motivation behind a poem which is pleasant both to the ear and to the eye. It reflects Hardy's ability not only to fashion out of memory the importance of loss, but also to make poetry out of the simple domestic occurrences that are the major part of life.

Nobody Comes

Another poem written in old age. It shows a remarkably keen observation, particularly in the description of the telegraph wire. And the repetition of the word 'spectral' shows that Hardy himself is still haunted by the past. Although this was written well after his second marriage, the sense of isolation, of being cut off from the experience of life, is very apparent in the final lines of the poem. The telegraph and the car have come into the land, but the effect of something coming and going means the negation of humanity, of what is permanent, perhaps, in country tradition. Although telegraph wires provide a means of communication, the sight of them on a lonely road seems to emphasize our own sense of isolation.

Intones to travellers like a spectral lyre Note how Hardy's ear has caught keenly the actual noise of the wires.
whangs Again an accurate, onomatopoeic effect is produced.
mute Conveys simply the lack of communication between man and the man-made: the wire and the car.

Night in the Old Home

Again the haunting of the past, this time the many ancestors instead of the 'woman much missed'. The long lines of the verses reflect the length of life and the backward-looking area spanned by memory. The theme is quite clearly a sense of his own difference from his ancestors, in the sense that they took life as it came; whereas he has questioned it and has expressed his doubts. The last verse is particularly effective, with the single words, in two batches of three, defining the ancestral view.

My perished people i.e. those from the distant past, the dead.
A pale late plant A reflection of his age: their 'final' descendant.
which consigns men to night A reference to his own cynicism.
fevered i.e. we did not fret and worry over things that did not concern us.

A Private Man on Public Men

A poetic exercise in the assumed voice of the man who has withdrawn from public life, written in the comparatively unusual form for Hardy of the rhyming couplet.

the Senate Parliament.

The Superseded

This poem focuses as Hardy so often does, on what is a commonplace: the feeling in age that younger people have overtaken and passed you despite your own feeling that you can continue and have much to offer. There is a note of bitterness in the first two verses, but this gives way to regret, a regret that is ironic in view of what Hardy was still to achieve in verse.

unforetold A typical Hardy use of the negative, which here echoes the negation of being 'superseded'.

He Never Expected Much
(or) A Consideration (*A reflection*) on my eighty-sixth birthday

The consideration is once more a looking-back to childhood, and then pondering on the lessons life taught him then. The 'neutral-tinted haps', a kind of learning to live with happiness and suffering and preparing yourself to do so. This is what the poet feels he has learned, and what he has lived by.

'I Look Into My Glass'

Another superbly condensed poem, which describes the ageing of the body and yet the capacity of the heart to experience suffering as keenly as ever. It is beautifully balanced, beginning with the look in the mirror that reflects the 'wasting skin', this linking immediately with the expression of loneliness in the second verse (a reflection in a mirror is hardly companionship). The third verse asserts that Time 'part steals, lets part abide': in other words takes away the physical but leaves the emotional. In a small way this is a bold poem, enunciating what is an inviolable truth about the nature of age, with a wistful recognition that has a certain moving dignity. Note too the use of 'Would God'. Speech, as we have seen, often gives dramatic immediacy to a Hardy poem.

Afterwards

The poet here affects to foresee the aftermath of his own death, with his idea of what people will say, for example, of his attitude towards nature. The five quatrains, with alternate lines rhyming, have a sonorous effect, almost funereal in atmosphere and emphasis. There are some fine individual coinages by Hardy, together with minute observation and sense-awareness. Alliteration is heavy, as befits the mournful nature of the subject. There is, too, an undercurrent of wry recognition, perhaps best exemplified in the unanswered question at the end of three of the verses. The poem tells us much of Hardy the man.

tremulous The word conveys at once the idea of age and the temporary nature of life itself.

like wings/Delicate-filmed as new-spun silk Fine simile and epithets, which indicate the subtle beauty of the veins on a leaf.

eyelid's soundless blink/The dewfall hawk Again the minute observation, and the linking of movement in man and nature.

wind-warped Alliterative epithet which describes how the wind 'bends' the thorn bushes.

furtively Note the pathos of the word – the hedgehog can only travel safely in the dark.

stilled Another euphemism for death.

full-starred heavens ... this thought rise Notice the
description of the fullness of life in the universe, and the subtle
idea of a thought that 'rises' – like the moon. This kind of
association is part of the imaginative structure of the poem.

Revision questions on poems mainly autobiographical

1 Write an essay on Hardy's use of the past and the present
in any *two* of the poems in this section.

2 Indicate the part played by nature in interaction with
personal relationships in any *two* or *three* of Hardy's poems.

3 Write an account of any *theme* present in Hardy's poems
in this section, and show how he presents it.

4 In what ways is nostalgia an important element in Hardy's
poetry? You should quote from a number of poems in
support of your views.

5 Consider Hardy's use of two or more verse forms, and
write an essay of appreciation, saying how they affect his
treatment of the subject about which he is writing.

6 Write an appreciation of any two poems that deal with
childhood in this section.

7 Discuss Hardy's use of irony in any two or three poems
here.

8 Show how Hardy presents commonplace moments or
incidents in his verse. You should refer to two or more poems
in your answer.

9 Write an essay on Hardy's treatment of the 'might-have-
been' in his verse.

10 In what way do you find Hardy's poetry cynical? *or* Write
an essay on 'lovingkindness' in his verse.

Incidents and Stories

The Pine Planters
(Marty South's reverie)

A fine lyrical poem in four-line verse in the first section and twelve-line stanzas in the second, though in effect they share the same length of line and rhythmic regularity. The first part is an imaginative identification of Marty South's love for Giles Winterborne. The first publication (in 1903) made no mention of Marty; the second section deals with a strong empathy between man (or woman here) and nature, an identification which, it must be stressed, runs throughout *The Woodlanders*, at least in the characters of Giles and Marty. The first section of 'The Pine Planters' is a controlled inward monologue, its main burden being one person's lack of awareness of the other, although they are working together in close proximity. As we have seen in the previous poems, this theme has been fully orchestrated by Hardy on a personal domestic level. The second section here deals with the planting of a tree and its developing of a 'voice' – the imaginative implication being that we, and nature, grow up into suffering. The fullness of the identification is ironic: the tree cannot move or speak; it can only endure. There is a fine alliterative 'song' throughout; and the poem gives the impression of being astutely balanced: a comment on life and love, with a final aside on old age too. The personification of the tree is undertaken in the language of studied understatement; suffering is the lot of man and nature, both being exposed to the 'storms' of life.

welter Rolling, hurly-burly.
halt Lamed, crippled.

Tess's Lament

Another poem of sadness in love, and again derived from the situation in one of his own novels, here the speaker being the heroine of *Tess of the d'Urbervilles*. The metrical treatment is very important, for the repetition, running into the second line, conveys the rocking motion to which Goss refers, almost as if the speaker is swaying to and fro in the anguish of utterance. The 'lament' is in character, for Tess's capacity to blame herself is part of that fullness of nature which makes her baptize her child Sorrow on the one hand and kill her lover Alec d'Urberville on the other. The readers of the novel will recall the physical and emotional shock of her being hanged, and this gives to the poem a consciously ironic element. The poignancy and the desolation are finely conveyed in the simple, insistent expression.

And no more see the sun Ironically, this is to be her 'lot'.
nook Secluded place.
within the chimney-seat Very ironically used here, since Tess even then sat out of the light, secluded (see 'nook' above) but was 'found out' (just as her past is 'found out' later).
The flowers we potted Note the immediate parallel with nature – the dead flowers, the 'dead' love.
dock Coarse, weedy herb.
it was I who did it all For readers of the novel, the irony once more – Tess is blameless in the true sense of the word.
guile Deception.
my Cross Tess is, in effect, a martyr.
my fate as writ i.e. as laid down.
unbe Fine use of the negative involving irony – 'I'd rather not be'.

Boys Then and Now

A brief but telling song of innocence and experience. It captures, in four simple verses, that area of childhood belief in something which adulthood proved was false, and yet there remains to the man who was a child the innocence and the treasuring of that belief. The poem goes further, for the changes between the generations, the recognition of what has come to be called the 'generation gap' is implicit in the poem: it is a wise and simple assertion of an inviolable truth.

new trim i.e. fresh blossom.
old already A cynical record of what can often be the case: the son who knows more than, and is already superior to, his father.

At the Railway Station, Upway

Hardy is adept, as we have seen, at making poetry out of a moment that is either commonplace or grotesque or, as here, poignant. We don't even know if the little boy is the son of the convict, or whether he is trying to earn money by playing at being 'imprisoned' himself in poverty; or whether it is a moment of childish compassion for the man about to go to prison, an outward movement of the heart to shame the grown-ups. Strangely, it doesn't matter, for the whole scene is depicted with an ironic wry understanding that immediately registers with the reader. It is a small incident of human contact, the compassion and participation transcending the inherent sadness.

pitying Unusual form of the word, exactly conveying here the motivation of the little boy.
grimful glee Almost a paradox, but exactly showing the man's ironic appraisal of his own situation.

In a Waiting Room

Hardy was fascinated by the casual encounter, and a minute observation of it and its significance in the broader perspective of life, and once again the scene is set before a journey. The poem encompasses the changes in mood we experience as casual events affect us, and the verse form is adjusted to fit this. The movement of the poem is an outward one, from the bagman's calculations in the Bible to the real-life experience of the soldier and his wife, forever parting – the burden of adult life – and to the children's responses to what the writer had regarded as 'fly-blown'. This movement is from pessimism to optimism, to a faith in youth and its innocent delight as distinct from the worries of age. There is a strong Romantic attitude here towards youth and innocence.

suchwise bent An economical way of saying 'if they were so inclined'.

cypher i.e. calculate.

charmless scene Note the irony – the apathy – successfully conveyed by this choice of word.

A smear of tragedy The image connects with 'fly-blown': lives are tainted too.

Subdued to stone by strong endeavour Notice how the metaphor conveys the smooth surface of self-control over their inward suffering.

It rained on the skylight Note how the outside world contrasts with the sudden 'glory' spread by the children's joy in life.

The Bird-catcher's Boy

Fine ballad, the first part in the form of dialogue, and again a distinct underlining of the generation gap. Briefly, the boy objects to his father's way of earning a living, escapes from the 'cage' of home – from which the birds can't escape – and, on the night he is drowned, appears to return to touch the wires of the bird-cages, just as he had done before he left. Hardy is the master of such narrative – simple, poignant, humane *and* with narrative tension and dramatic effects: we want to know what happened. One of the major facets of Hardy's art is his ability to tell a story, whether it be in verse or prose, and here we find all the compassion of the boy and the anguish of the parents who have lost him. There is also a social and moral comment implicit in the two attitudes, that of father and son, towards the imprisoning of the birds; and we know that Hardy's sympathies lie beyond the job-necessity of the man.

dolt Fool.
pat Properly.
Lightless An uncommon word, here carrying a moral weight as well.
caged choirs i.e. the captured birds. Note that the musical image is echoed in the boy's action, an underlining of his sympathy with the birds – it is almost a caress.
wist Knew.
groping touch Note the effect of this word – conveying uncertainty – as distinct from the 'harp-like' touch of the boy when alive.
much Again the economical usage, here meaning 'much as if'.

A Wife Waits

Another short realistic capturing of a situation and an immediate imaginative and sympathetic identification with the speaker. The theme is the sudden cooling of love, the man returning to his old haunts. The comment embraces a sardonic look at marriages that are made in romance and die at the touch of reality: almost a poignant comment on Hardy's own marriage. It is a ballad, only three verses being needed to tell the story. There is even a sadness in the idea of the woman's constancy.

treading a tune i.e. dancing.
shivering Notice how effective this word is, emphasized by the rhythmic fall at the beginning of the line.

The Market-girl

Subtle variation in the two verses here, for the second incorporates an internal rhyme and the longer lines reflect the building of the relationship after the initial question. Again it is a commonplace enough situation, but here with the dressing of romance, not autobiographical of course, though the man does speak and his courtship begins. The might-have-been is translated into reality.

Throwing a Tree
(New Forest)

The four-line verses here are so handled that the longer fourth lines firstly presage the fall of the tree, then describe it; and reflect the long-drawn-out efforts of the men, as well as the time of the growing and falling that Hardy is so careful to stress. The identification with nature is so sympathetic that the actions of the men are *felt*, and what is a job becomes an event of importance. Both the technique and the contrast inherent in the poems might be studied by looking back at 'The Pine Planters' and comparing it with this poem. It would reveal Hardy's meticulous attention to the details of his verse forms and rhythms, even to the point of sound and movement.

axes Meant to remind us of historic executions.
the proud tree that bears the death-mark i.e. has been marked for 'execution', like so many diseased elms suffering from Dutch elm disease in our own time.
lie white on the moss There is a certain purity about the image, as if this is the 'blood' of a great independent virginal being.
gash Powerfully evocative of pain and suffering.
The saw then begins Notice how this verse, with its shorter lines initially, reflects the cutting movement.
the living mast Hardy is not unmindful of the associations with ships, and the word 'living' is particularly effective by way of stressing the contrast.

Job and Ike The two 'executioners'. It is almost as if they shudder at the destruction and the knowledge that their turn will come.

two hundred years ... two hours As we have seen, Hardy employs contrast, but with a telling humanity here; for history, tradition – two of Hardy's major themes – are broken in nature, which has the greatest history and tradition of all.

The Old Workman

The four-line verses have two rhyming lines, but the second pair is rounded off with a shorter end-stopped line. The poem contains some pathos on account of the injuries suffered by the workman, but there is a certain exalted tone as his pride in what he has achieved – for others – is described. Again, the poem begins as a dialogue, but settles into the one speaker's account. As few writers before him, Hardy was obviously conscious of the dignity of labour.

crookt i.e. bent.

walled from wind and rain The contrast is immediately apparent – the mason has spent his life unprotected from the elements, but what he builds is a protection for others.

They don't know me ... When I lie underground Apart from the sentiment of pride in one's work, there is also the moral implication that working to do good for others is the standard to live by. What is ironic is the lack of contact between the mason and the people he has built for – a lack of contact which we are aware of and dismiss, but which Hardy chooses to emphasize in this passing comment on life.

The Choirmaster's Burial

This is a further instance of Hardy's versatility in the use of form, for the lines are short and the rhymes are picked up almost like notes in music – an indication of the poet's achieving some degree of harmony with his subject. There is thus, though we are dealing with death, a lightness of touch – rather as if the ghostly choirmaster of the poem is himself conducting. This ghostly effect is at times tantalizing, but the theme of the poem is quite clearly the exercise of human response to a request. This contrasts with the practice of the Vicar, for he merely follows the ritual of Christian observance despite the known wish of the dead man.

task us i.e. be too much for us.
grave-brim Graveside, but unusually put.
To get through it faster A damning comment on the Vicar's christianity.
Like the saints in church-glass Comparing the essential 'earthly' or 'ghostly' saints with those who have a permanent place. There is also contrast with the Vicar.

The Sacrilege
(A Ballad-tragedy. About 182–)

A ballad divided into two parts, and only with the opening of Part 2 do we realize that the narrator is dead, and that the whole is informed therefore with a mysterious and macabre atmosphere. The story is quite straightforward: a man who robs a church for his mistress is caught in the act. Before he is hanged he places upon his brother the burden of revenge: should his rival, Wrestler Joe, take over his mistress, then the brother is to kill her. The narrative is brilliantly sustained, rich in local atmosphere and colour, with a running repetition of the landmarks throughout. Places visited, dialect echoes, visual pictures and a mastery of dialogue all play their part in what is essentially a dramatic narrative. Mention has been made earlier of Hardy's story-telling ability; and this poem and the three following ones – in which the horrible, the pathetic, the tragic and the supernatural all play a part – are testimony to that ability. One sees here Hardy's working of the mines of folklore and legend; with an awareness of his own roots, those of the hearth, the fireside with the stories of the elders. Perhaps the greatest common factor of appeal in each of these poems is the dramatic immediacy Hardy achieves through the simple recital – in each case the teller of the tale is intimately involved in the action, and the reader shares fears, hopes, even actions and reactions. In the first poem the verses are of eight lines, with a repeated word as rhyme in the first and third, and a triple rhyme in the second half of each verse. Personification – for instance of Dunkery – and alliteration abound throughout.

gallanting The *English Dialect Dictionary* gives this as 'gay, roving, roaming', but the implication is 'keeping company with, courting'.

Dunkery frowns This is repeated, and is a natural, ominous symbol, as if they are fated.

swift sweets outwore i.e. the happy times passed.

beauties bright as tulips blown i.e. her lips.

van i.e. caravan.

sloe-black Sudden economical coinage: black sloes are ripe, and give added depth (and temptation) to her eyes.

dallyings i.e. flirtation.

finger Steal.

mart Market.

I've stayed my hand i.e. I have drawn the line, refused to steal.

Curbed by a law not of the land i.e. superstitious fear.

pouts Note the immediate connection with nature.

my soul's imperilling i.e. that I shall go to hell.

who is my ravishing i.e. seduces me by her charm.

botchery ... assay Making a mess of ... this rash attempt.

bedwinner Fine coinage, an obvious verbal echo of the common 'breadwinner'.

Born at my birth i.e. his twin.

Or one more foul i.e. his evil spirit.

ill-witchery ... lure of eyes There is a sexual and a supernatural implication here.

And yet I could not bear i.e. to do what he had been asked to do.

figure i.e. appear.

clave ... cleaves i.e. the natural association again. The word means 'stuck fast to'.

Your goodman's The implication of the brother is that Wrestler Joe may have drowned.

such might bode What it meant.

undue i.e. untimely.

He sees ... Until his judgement-time There is a compulsive guilt about this, somewhat reminiscent of the Ancient Mariner's in Coleridge's poem of that name.

A Trampwoman's Tragedy
(182–)

Again the story in outline is a simple one; two wandering couples, with the narrator flirting with the other man and in a rash moment falsely admitting that he is the father of her coming child. Her lover thereupon kills the man, is hanged for it; and the woman (having had a still-born child), sees her lover's ghost. Thereafter it is she who continues to haunt the Western Moor. The eight-line verse is employed, but with the variant of a short second line, and a similar use of repetition as a refrain. This adds substantially to the building up of an emotional atmosphere. Hardy is very good at conveying primitive passion and impulsiveness in these ballad stories.

turnpike tracks Presumably following the old road, which would have a toll-gate on it for the payment of a tax.

landskip sights i.e. (the best) view: in this case the inn.

O deadly day i.e. an ill-fated one.

at last we won i.e. climbed.

and Mother Lee/Passed to my former one An early form of itinerant wife-swapping, or mistress-swapping, as the case may be.

Gilded ... glazing Note the colour and the heavy alliteration, which reflect the deed.

swung i.e. was hanged.

stained i.e. he had only one other crime: the stealing of a horse when he needed it.

death-day ... dead-born Note the effectiveness of the repetition, and the macabre, supernatural coincidence implied.

and thinned away The words convey the ghostly 'fading'.

A Sunday Morning Tragedy
(about 186–)

This time the poem is in a straightforward ballad form with alternate lines rhyming, and the narrator is the mother of the tragic heroine of the tale. Finding her daughter pregnant, she pleads with the man to marry her and, on his refusal to do so, the mother consults a shepherd about a herbal method of abortion. She tries it and then, when her daughter is taken ill, finds that the lover is prepared to marry the girl after all. They find the girl dead when they go to see her.

flower-fair Simple epithet, later to be ironically echoed in 'picotee'.

joyed Note the unusual, rhythmically fitting verbal usage.

plodded ... pleaded Part of the running alliteration used by Hardy.

to sail the main i.e. go to sea.

Though better I had ceased It would have been better if I had not done so.

'Or none?' A pathetic indication that the mother knows she is doing wrong – hoping for an answer that will tell her there is no herb that can bring about the abortion.

The sunset-shine Brilliantly ironic, since the shepherd, normally associated with good, is here the bringer of evil.

baulk i.e. prevent.

Why should they be? The question is again indicative of the mother's unhappiness at going against nature by using the herb, but the voice is Hardy's own.

poppling Tossing, rippling.

wind whiffled wailfully i.e. nature is already mourning the coming deed: 'whiffled' means slight movements of air or wind.

lours Scowls, frowns.

fond salute i.e. loving greeting.

betimes Early.

raiment ... sackcloth-clad Note the immediate contrast: the outward showing-off at church; and the garments of penitence.

bantered Joked, teased.

Death had took her ... Death took not me Note the effective contrast: the living suffer on.

colding A fine word to indicate the onset of death, the gradual disappearance of life.

***not* to pity me** Her sense of guilt and remorse is such that she does not want to be pardoned by God. The tragedy is as much hers as her daughter's.

The Lost Pyx
(A Medieval Legend)

In this poem, which covers the areas of the Christian and the supernatural, Hardy makes great use of internal rhyme and an insistent rhythm. Although the legend has another less pleasant version, the one given here sounds, for a change, a note of optimism. One night a priest hears a call telling him to go and shrive a man who is dying. He ignores it at first, but after seeing a visage frowning down on him from Heaven, he sets out through the terrible night only to find, when he arrives at the home of the dying man, that the pyx containing the Holy Sacrament is missing. He turns back on his tracks and finds the pyx on a hill, surrounded by all the worshipping animals of nature. The priest returns to the cottage, where he kneels in prayer, and gives the last rites to the dying man. Later, he has a stone raised in memory of the occasion.

Attests i.e. bears witness to.

trees twanged We have seen that Hardy is greatly observant of the noise and movement of the trees, and the onomatopoeic effect here reflects the stormy night.

in hail i.e. within calling distance.

And head in a heat of shame Superbly simple, economical description to underline his feelings.

freight i.e. the Pyx.

won place i.e. became the sub-prior.

Revision questions on Incidents and Stories

1 Compare and contrast any *two* of the longer poems in this section, bringing out clearly Hardy's story-telling ability and the verse techniques he uses.

2 By a study of any *two* or *three* poems in this section, show how Hardy makes poetry out of a moment or an incident.

3 Write an essay on Hardy's use of *pathos* in any selection of poems from this group, and say whether or not you find his work moving.

4 Write a considered appreciation of Hardy's use of nature in any *three* of the poems in this section.

5 In what ways do the poems in this section reflect Hardy's compassion and humanity? You may refer to any three or four poems in your answer.

6 Write an essay on the variety of *form* used by Hardy in *either* the shorter *or* the longer poems in this section.

Descriptive and Animal Poems

Weathers

This poem of two verses – the eight lines of the narrative poems being extended here to nine – has three effective short lines to six longer ones evocative of the contrasting weather. It is full of natural observation and a direct appraisal of the way our moods are conditioned by the weather, the refrain linking the poet with the reactions of common humanity, thus giving to the verse the 'universality' which has been noted as one of the major achievements of Hardy's mature art. The interlocking rhymes common to both stanzas emphasize Hardy's concept of the unity of nature.

betumble Poetic word for 'set them falling'.
nestlings i.e. young birds just capable of flying.
little brown nightingale Note the effect of this description: the small simplicity of the bird contrasted with the beauty of the song. Think back to *The Darkling Thrush*.
And rooks in families Note the identification of man with nature yet again.

Before and After Summer

A simple and economically expressed poem in a conversational tone, written in couplets varied by alternate-line rhyming, marking clearly the passage of time in retrospect, but noting, with an ironic self-awareness, that summer has gone – and passed unnoticed at the time. The universal truth is that what we look forward to for so long passes almost before we are aware of it.

wintry scourgings i.e. the sufferings brought by winter.
a half-transparent blind The implication is that the sun will

emerge, but the idea of the blind seems to convey also the fact that we hide behind the 'blinds' of our houses in bad weather.

Blank as I am even is he Once more the identification of man with nature, the inverted word order reflecting the lack of animation.

I, alas, perceived not when There is a poignant sense of time lost in this last line.

A Backward Spring

Here the emphatic mood is stressed by an account of the late arrival of spring, and the poem is built on an intimate personification seen in the reactions of nature to this arresting of the cycle. The personal qualities – fear, timidity, worry – are transferred to the trees, grass and bushes, and the second half of the poem focuses on the myrtle, the final lines going back to its survival in the winter. Again the alternate-line rhyming is varied by couplets and shorter lines.

And the primrose pants Note the sense of 'pace' in nature and hence the importance of time in its due season.

Though the myrtle asks The shrub with shiny evergreen leaves and the white flowers to which Hardy refers as 'buttons'.

'If It's Ever Spring Again'
(Song)

A lyric evocative of romance and the past, the two seasons of the year, summer and spring, that are associated with love and with the stirring and movement of nature. The refrain gives an intentional lightness of touch. The references to love ('Standing with my arm around her') are nostalgic and senti-mental, and there is a wistful air about the poem: a song written for singers in chorus rather than there being any personal involvement. This, however, does not detract from its lilting charm.

amid their flounder i.e. as they are floundering about.
the cuckoos-two-in rhyme They symbolize romantic love.
achime i.e. in harmony.

An Unkindly May

Just as Hardy is the recorder of the commonplace moment,
with an elevation of his own that turns it into poetry, so he
is the recorder of the commonplace in nature, but with a rare
eye for detail. The fact that this is an 'unkindly May' is shown
in the metrical heaviness of the lines, which are thus consonant
with a mood that would normally be much brighter and
lighter. The whole has the effect of a painting.

blurting boisterous-wise Heavy alliteration to emphasize the
 scene.
like rusty cranes The simile conveys the 'unkindliness' of the
 month, the man-made parallel emphasizing it in view of Hardy's
 known affection for things natural rather than for man's
 mechanical trappings.
eye-trying flaps i.e. because the sudden shafts of sunlight are
 only occasionally seen in passing.
commendable i.e. not worthy of praise (while you are in this
 state).
That shepherd still stands Again the view of man against the
 landscape, the unchanging nature of rustic habit and time.

An August Midnight

Two simple six-line verses, consisting of a quatrain with two
alternate lines rhyming and a couplet in each verse, in which
the poet contemplates insect-life – its knowledge, its lore, its
ritual – with its store of experience of which he can know
nothing. It is a strangely moving poem, as small and complete
in its compass as is the insect life described.

that rubs its hands The personification here indicates Hardy's minute observation of habit, and invests the unprotected creature with a certain pathos.

They know Earth-secrets The term is capitalized and hyphenated in order to show the largeness (to itself) of the world of the 'humblest': each creature, however small, leads a life unknown to man.

Shortening Days at the Homestead

The early Autumn days are captured here in fourteen lines – though not a sonnet – of varying line-length and a fine figurative flow. The second part opens with a question which has all the expectancy of a time loved particularly for its associations – the cider season, redolent of excitement and picking, has arrived.

The first fire since the summer Note the length of the line, equivalent to the slow rising of smoke after the long summer.

Sparrows spurt Alliterative effect that conveys the speed of movement.

whom misgivings appal i.e. they are apprehensive, for the autumn signals the coming return of winter – they having thought that winter had gone forever. One of Hardy's imaginative associations.

Like shock-headed urchins, spiny-haired A fine image, again linking man and nature in an unexpected way.

pondering pace Again the alliteration reflects the movement – the slow tread.

embossed i.e. standing out (he is white-headed).

mill i.e. for grinding the apples, an old-fashioned liquidizer.

The Later Autumn

Three verses, again showing human and detailed observation of nature at a certain time of the year. The short lines contrast with the longer ones, and there is a lightness of touch despite the season of the year, almost as if the poet delights in recording what he sees. There is only one sombre note, which is struck at the end of the second verse where the shades are compared to 'lives soon to end'.

the line of your track i.e. your direction.
Leg-laden i.e. because they are loaded with pollen.
Spinning leaves ... On whose corpses The fine personification conveys the life-cycle of nature, the irony of death being apparent: for the 'scorners' are already falling.
A robin looks on An almost optimistic hint of the coming of winter.

Last Week in October

This opens with a fine personification of the trees 'undressing', and then sharpens down to focus on the spider's web — another manifestation in small and deadly compass. Again the contrast in the appearance and practice of nature is central to the effects achieved by the poet.

radiant robes This is redolent of the colours of autumn.
Here, there Note the repetition in this line – a reflection of the movement of the leaves.
Like a suspended criminal hangs he The image is one that strongly influenced Hardy who, as a child, witnessed a hanging from a distance.
as fearing a fate The unobtrusive personification of the leaves shows Hardy's ever-present idea of the *living* quality of nature.

The Last Chrysanthemum

These perennials can bloom into December. The verses – quatrains – are lyrically balanced, but the contemplation of this small aspect of nature is enhanced by a strongly spiritual ending that is almost pantheistic in its emphasis. It is a mature, consummately planned poem, the small and great encompassed in its tone and in its seeing into the 'hidden harmony' of things.

flower ... tombs Note at once the contrast – life and death – which so often occurs in Hardy's verse.

leaves like corpses See the note above, for this lyric is also funereal. 'In the midst of life we are in death' applies to the natural cycle as well as to that of man.

season's shine There is much alliteration in this poem, and it makes for a kind of music.

witlessness The three-syllabled word conveys vacancy, a lack of thought.

stay its stress Delay its trials, hardships.

one mask ... the Great Face An acknowledgement of an omniscient Being, the inscrutable mystery behind all things.

Winter Night in Woodland
(Old Time)

Four six-line verses which move from nocturnal activity in nature to the bird-baiters and poachers; then to the 'land-carriers' employed by the smugglers; and finally to the choir. The names will be familiar to readers of Hardy's novel *Under the Greenwood Tree*.

As from teachings of years i.e. the result of his experiences, and of the experiences of the fox family.

death-halloo Hardy is binding the cry of the fox-hunters to that of the fox hunted down and killed.

worn carols i.e. timeworn, used through the generations.

they home Another elliptical construction, eliminating 'go'.

Ice on the Highway

A human, even humorous, moment: a particular experience captured and set down with a fine awareness of the atmosphere but not neglecting the women's need to buy food. The verse 'slips' into lines consonant with the physical uncertainty of the conditions. There is a good sense of the give-and-take of the enforced companionship.

stagger Note also the 'staggering' rhythm of this poem.

Snow in the Suburbs

Description of a scene, the interesting treatment consisting of selective detail and control of a rhythm exactly reflecting for example, the wayward movement of the snowflakes. This control is extended to the heavier movement of snow which nearly entombs a sparrow; then there is a finely controlled ending: attenuated lines that correspond to the size and move- ment of the cat.

like a white web-foot Fine natural association, showing Hardy's keen eye.

Some flakes have lost their way The longer lines reflect the desultory movement of the flakes.

glued together like a wall This accurately defines in terms of texture the icy hardness, impenetrability, of the conditions. It is, too, a powerful tactile image.

the fleecy fall Again an appropriate association, since thick snow provides warmth, as does the wool of the sheep.

And overturns him All things in nature are relative – the 'lump', small to us, is mountainous to the sparrow.

nether Lower.

Starts off a volley Notice how the rhythm of the line captures the movement of the snow.

And we take him in As often with Hardy, the essentially human element is included: the sparrow survives, and the cat must too, here with the aid of man.

To a Tree in London
(Clement's Inn)

Short lines in triplets, sounding a pathetic note since the tree never lives among its kind but among the streets and buildings that are not its natural companions. The roots of the tree are compared to the movable roots of man; and the effect conveyed, for once in Hardy, is of a deprivation in nature.

Smoke like earth An ironic way of describing the dirty air.
a blue immense i.e. suggestive of freedom.

The Fallow Deer at the Lonely House

This superb little poem sharply focuses on the lack of correspondence between the conditions of beast and man: the latter within, in comfort; the former without, perhaps lonely. It is a moment of magical imagination, the concept going beyond sentiment because of the fine discrimination in choice of words; the single associations of the last two lines being particularly effective in setting up in the reader's consciousness a sympathetic bond with the subject of the poem. Nowhere is Hardy's humanitarian concern for animals and his imaginative identification with their state seen to better advantage. The poem is as finely structured as a lovingly created building, as beautiful in symmetry as the deer itself.

discern Stronger than 'see', because the eye of the imagination is being used all the time. It implies 'see with the mind'.
Wondering Each word here is weighted with a sympathetic sense: the unknown thoughts of the animal; the natural glow of life; the creature; and the 'tiptoe' which imparts a pathetic air of loneliness.

The Faithful Swallow

A brief lyrical lament, in short lines, the poet identifying with the one bird that did not leave at the appointed time. It is a slight poem, one however that shows the usual control of the chosen form. The lines here, in their lightness and ease of sense and rhyme, almost convey the movements of the bird's wings.

As fickle they! i.e. as false as (my companions).
Fidelity i.e. loyalty.

The Robin

This poem is like that above, in that it employs a very similar technique throughout, though this one is a poem of contrasts. There is keen observation of the habits of the robin, and an exactitude in recording sound. Notice how effective is the use of the robin as narrator.

I see in pools i.e. the reflection (of the sky) in the pools.
earth as steel Again one is forced to note the effective economy of the expression.

The Puzzled Game-birds
(Triolet)

A moving short poem, which is admirably covered by the note. The form is, as we should expect, finely handled, with a plaintive and poignant reiteration of man's inhumanity to the birds he intends to use.

The Blinded Bird

Another moving poem, strongly linked in theme to the previous one. To remove one faculty is often to strengthen another, but the superbly used biblical associations of the last verse speak of the divinity of a complete thing. The repetition of the simple 'This bird' at the beginning and end of the verse is an example of a sureness of touch. The two words recall the sublimity, the miracle, of Creation.

With God's consent Note the irony.
that stab of fire i.e. the red-hot needle.
Enjailed in pitiless wire i.e. a bird-cage.
ensepulchred i.e. buried alive.

Horses Aboard

Again an identification, this time with horses being transported to a war overseas. The appraisal is cynical – they are being used – and the lines are long, in order to reflect the sombreness of the poet's mood as he contemplates horses being moved from 'the scheme Nature planned for them'. This poem might be compared with 'Drummer Hodge'.

ghast i.e. ghastly.

A Sheep Fair

Two stanzas and a postscript, the form rather similar to that employed in 'Weathers' in terms of length of line, but the emphasis in the first two stanzas here is atmospheric, descriptive, while the postscript is a comment on the passage of time.

with tucked-in tails i.e. because the dogs are wet and miserably inactive.
Going – going! Note the irony: the words are a comment on all that is gone, including the auctioneer himself.
mewed band Confined.

The Roman Gravemounds

Quatrains, with alternate lines rhyming, a finely ironic comment on the past and its greatness, man's simple qualities (love of animals) in the present; yet the linking of past and present is in the expression of humanity. The irony early in the poem is a piece of self-exposure, but the poet moves on to contemplate man's ignorance of greatness and his simple expression of grief. It is a movement of the heart against the tide of history: the Hardy of domestic love, with animals as friends.

scan i.e. search.
regard i.e. estimate.

Last Words to a Dumb Friend

This is perhaps the most expressive of Hardy's animal poems, with superb control of touch; and one is tempted to say that there is a sleekness about the verse that approximates to the sleekness of the poem's subject. It exists on two levels, that of the finely descriptive on one hand, and of the contemplative, wry, ironical on the other. The fluency derives in part from an expert handling of the octosyllabic couplets.

Foot suspended in its fall Note the way that Hardy has captured the actual pose of the cat.
Never another pet Note here the anti-romantic, anti-sentimental attitude, more redolent of grief than any outward show could be.
Strange it is The whole verse is given over to the contemplation of the reversal of positions – the cat, dependent on its masters in life, yet registers as the Imperturbable in death. Hardy goes on to describe how the house itself 'Grows all eloquent of him' after he has gone.
That you moulder where you played The final comment is ironic in tone – the death of the body, the linking of life past, death present, on the same spot.

Dead 'Wessex' the Dog to the Household

The poem has a certain poignancy but even an imaginative projection into the supposed words of the dog cannot save it from some bathos – though perhaps this is deliberate. Three lines of repetition do not help to raise the level of the verse, which never reaches that of the previous poem.

as 'twere i.e. as if it were mine.

'Ah, Are You Digging on My Grave?'

A poem cleverly divided into two main parts, the words of the dead loved one and the words of the living dog. The comment is ironic, for it calls to account the whole question of the remembrance of the dead. Here both man and dog are found wanting; for the man marries another and the dog was burying a bone where his mistress has her (apparently) far from *resting* place. Terms like 'dig' and 'rest' have thus their own ironic force, and the poem is much more than its outward form, for it is almost a parody of the elegy which pays tribute to the dead. Relations and enemies alike are wholly indifferent; and the comment is that time changes everything: loyalty, love, the memory. The language is simple, for the qualities named in the previous sentence are simple ones. But the poet's appraisal of these qualities tells him that man does what he wants to do, and that the past is soon burned out in the present.

Revision questions on Descriptive and Animal Poems

1 Write an appreciation of any *two* of Hardy's descriptive poems, indicating the main techniques he employs.

2 By close attention to any *two* or *three* poems in this section, write an essay on Hardy's use of contrast.

3 Which do you find the most moving poem in this section and why? Write a detailed appreciation of it.

4 In what ways does Hardy make his love of animals clear? In your answer you should look closely at *three* poems.

5 In what ways could Hardy's description of nature *or* his writing of animals be described as ironic? Quote in support of your views, referring to a number of poems in your answer.